Sun Cycle

Recent Cleveland State University Poetry Center publications:

Poetry
The Hartford Book by Samuel Amadon
The Grief Performance by Emily Kendal Frey
My Fault by Leora Fridman
Orient by Nicholas Gulig
Stop Wanting by Lizzie Harris
Vow by Rebecca Hazelton
Age of Glass by Anna Maria Hong
The Tulip-Flame by Chloe Honum
Render / An Apocalypse by Rebecca Gayle Howell
A Boot's a Boot by Lesle Lewis
In One Form to Find Another by Jane Lewty
50 Water Dreams by Siwar Masannat
daughterrarium by Sheila McMullin
The Bees Make Money in the Lion by Lo Kwa Mei-en
Residuum by Martin Rock
Festival by Broc Rossell
The Firestorm by Zach Savich
Mother Was a Tragic Girl by Sandra Simonds
I Live in a Hut by S.E. Smith
Bottle the Bottles the Bottles the Bottles by Lee Upton
Adventures in the Lost Interiors of America by William D. Waltz
Uncanny Valley by Jon Woodward
You Are Not Dead by Wendy Xu

Essays
I Liked You Better Before I Knew You So Well by James Allen Hall
A Bestiary by Lily Hoang
The Leftovers by Shaelyn Smith

Translation
I Burned at the Feast: Selected Poems of Arseny Tarkovsky translated by Philip Metres and Dimitri Psurtsev

For a complete list of titles visit www.csupoetrycenter.com

Sun Cycle

Anne Lesley Selcer

Cleveland State University Poetry Center
Cleveland, Ohio

Printed in the United States of America
Printed on acid-free paper

ISBN: 978-0-914946-09-0

First edition

23 22 21 20 19 5 4 3 2 1

This book is published by the Cleveland State University Poetry Center,
2121 Euclid Avenue, Cleveland, Ohio 44115-2214
www.csupoetrycenter.com and is distributed by
SPD / Small Press Distribution, Inc. www.spdbooks.org.

Cover image: *Kestnermappe Proun, Rob. Levnis and Chapman GmbH Hannover #5*, El Lissitzky
Cover design: Amy Freels
Sun Cycle was designed and typeset by Amy Freels in Futura.

A catalog record for this title is available from the Library of Congress.

You gaze at m/e with your ten thousand eyes, you do so and it is I, I do not stir, m/y feet are completely embedded in the ground, I allow m/yself to be reached by your ten thousand glances or if you prefer by the single glances of your ten thousand eyes but it is not the same, such an immense gaze touches m/e everywhere, I hesitate to move, if I raise m/y arms toward the sun you slant your eyes to adjust to the light, they sparkle but you look at m/e or else if I should move into the shade I am cold your eyes are not visible there where you follow m/e I too am unseen by you, I am dumb in this desert devoid of your ten thousand eyes darker than the dark where your eyes would appear to m/e ten-thousand fold black and shining, I am alone until the moment when I hear a variety of sounds of bells of tintinnabulations, I tremble, I am giddy, it reverberates within m/e, it makes m/e quiver, it is the music of the eyes I say to m/yself, either they clash together gently and with violence or they produce these many sounds by themselves, I fling m/yself flat on my face in front or behind this side or that, I gesticulate wildly to learn that I cannot escape the multiplicity of your regard, wherever I may be my ineffable one you gaze at m/e with your ten thousand eyes.

Monique Wittig

Appearing

You awaken to ornate, administrative violence,
a hundred boy eyed arpeggios,
a hundred sunsets which refer to contemporary forms,
a hundred messages or inscriptions bleached in white noise,
to what always remains absolutely incapable of forming a representation,
to interiority without escape,
a hundred tomes which fan out into the negation of the passage of time,
a black hundred concatenations, an incommunicable hundred bodies.
You awaken on screen to everything you could ever want;
it repeats, recapitulates, laps like the goddamn waves,
like a hundred humid, dispersing forms of light
under a thick dust in tumult
turning a contrapuntal hundred somersaults.
You awaken to these sensations you're hosting,
you awaken to the most normal, American thing,
you awaken and lose the right to your body,
to the exquisite subjugation which is the notion of taste,
you awaken inside another's mouth.

In a system of ons and offs
in the silent language of lighthouses
in an inconsequential, feminine swarm—

An unaccountable beauty

fecund but not sacred
walks alone along a street in New York City
past a pile of commodity, Italianate, reproductive, rotting,
past a gallery of caryatids,
past girls manipulating the nobs of a cathartic art,
past canephora bearing transactions in their baskets,
past a vanishing metaphysical realm,
the bird, the vase, the book, unable now to justify
or account for the weight of their own beauty,
past machines blowing bubbles in a room walled with mirrors
past day ladies speaking of their travels,
the light kindly buoying the undersides of their public play,
past a chamber of chaste girls encased in silver
and looking through mirrors of chrysolite, carbuncle, sapphire, and emerault,
past a million images of the self, venerated, fed back to the self,
past the notion of photographic absence, then the real disappeared,
past Walt Whitman's pile of limbs,
past buildings falling, caryatids with broken necks,
past a mass of metal, a tract of land, a number of slaves,
a pile of stones, a human body of certain lineaments,
past a solid wall of caryatids, an army—
"Oh, the young girl, that receptacle of shameful secrets
sealed in her own beauty!"

Bye gash

taken like glitter is taken, by mistake, surplus beauty adheasing to every surface which once you let go, just goes; industry springing up inside time and history. Bye gash hacked open by your own vitality, useless beauty whom industry springs up around. Goodbye language, or hello.

Stretch a swath of saturnine afternoon across a season's memory. Disappear into the predictable industrial morning. Take out every labor, polish it dutifully. Smash the glass. Bigger, please. You are carefully surviving what needs to be destroyed. I need you to language otherwise.

Pollen

An accelerated alphabet
a mumbled picture

a ridiculous fluorescence of page after page
peacocked on a green screen

as if each term flagrantly raised an objection
against its own denotative power

under local clouds

now it's your turn to fall down
from the love of the look

that turned politics to puddles
turned it to feathers

slowed it to pollen
slowed it to oil which shimmers in a slick

a scriptio continua an angel wrote
then threw like a parachute into thin air

each corner held down by a small child
who, unemployed and not yet signified, sings,

"empire is everywhere nothing happens
everywhere everything happens at once."

Before we were filled with content, we sought to be filled with sensation

beauty is a particular unit of duration
the day is a palace, each hour a room
is a form of sadness

is a deferral of the movement of time

evening dawning on the housetops
the sky an impossible screen

is circular, complete
decorated with silver embossed leaves

is an object
an hour of the eyes

moves out of a warm, general indisputability
into a contraction which is form

exists as a cold, hard public specificity
a positive presence in a market of exchange

is posterior to perception
silver to gold

is the inferior or the primary currency
the king has this alchemical ability

there are one hundred ways to ornament a note.

Fronding and intricate, ruined with color

if property creates meaning,
a landlord is a baroque and overgenerative thing.
Pigment stacked into tall rows,
permanence and significance,
terrestrial plentitude and distribution,
color slung into rings.
Ownership is abstraction's embrace.
This dynamic female form,
pink washed at the bottom,
green escaping its line;
if the terms of the social are the limits of the social
is it beauty before it's privatized?
The world of abstraction is a world of surfaces,
they are its only sociality.
As for correspondences,
"The administration said send two,
which we refused.
I said we should all go."

My mother was a secret house

a new round of enclosures,
Adriatic, Galia, Algerian, Atago,

magic renamed refusal,
Bella Heart, Betty Anne, Bergamot, Black,

Black Amber, Black Beauty, Black Globe, Black Pearl,
unchained and disenchanted,

Angel, Aprium, Arkansas Black,
Athena, Baldwin, apricot,

sex transformed into work,
Black Current, Black Rochelle, Baby Bear,

Catalina, Cherimoya, Crimson Red,
Crab Apple, Clementina, Crimson Glow,

repulsion and complicity, ostracism and negation,
Red Delicious, Dancy, D'Anjou Red,

Ellendale, Crimson, Crimson Sweet,
medicines reformulated into perfumes.

In Elephant Heart, Barhi, Black Raspberry,
Black Sugarcane, Canaydria, Canary,

Bartlett, Babcock, Blackberry,
Calimyrna, Cello Blood,

Ariran, Athena, Amagaki,
my mother was a feral house.
Ambrosia, Apple Pear.

Command poem

Empire, defend yourself. Mold material form.

Form a line of lights. Make dead skin of commodity.

Chime the clang original. Take care, predator.

Be raw tin rain. Her voice, always signify.

Black sand, circle and sludge. Where'd her voice go?

Into unnecessary, technological terror.

Delete, in succession each part of your body.

Lay down enemy. Your life becomes economy.

Store a whole American body in your negativity.

Gild poverty. Negate any means of unification as you appear.

Appear not actually real.

Defend coastal paintbrush, false hellebore, wild valerian.

Defend entropy.

Meanwhile, in cold pink and silver rooms gold necklaces slip through female fingers—

solid mounds and maritime orchard time of slaves, noose hands that woman had, noose hands she had. Puffed full blown and well-disposed to cocktail clutter and books of rose, maritime rose, her bible pinks heavy, black as that, her pinks were black as that. Janus faced and jackal souled, a slivering of knifeshade straight down the gills, and apple hands and thrilled and trilled.

The soil is

an aporia in the middle of the mother's mouth.
Her eyes are negated by a searing solar interior
whose blankness asserts,
each object is involved in its own perpetual dawning,
every object emerges by way of its own negation in light.

Then there, across the bridge
where ebullience turns on permanent emergency,
a synthetic sublime,
reproduction in its relentlessness,
financialized colors create new colors,
thus new relationships with light.

Look at her hair, in waves.
Her medium drops
into the center of the era,
a dead, beautiful stone.

What if I were to click on her—
how far down does death go, I wonder,
into being the opposite of a mother?

too present in meanings whilst I walk in and amongst the shops. My tree, my pinnacle, my cloudlike. When winning took the form of femininity described to me from four angles and roaring forward with many low-paid attendants. The bad facts or untrustworthy ones, the habit of luminous noise: Oh brightening field, oh city street, oh capital and forgetful cloak, oh row of screens, a fire on each. The promise of the city to a person like me; gone turning on the wheel, familiar as family. Was fear outside the house, actually lurking there? I counted the ways in which I could become interior. I understood hair as raw material, formed a habit of hiding in representation's fold. Now here is an object, now air must flow around it, seen because it gathers light, a cloak of mirror; this is the information by which the civis knows me. Come to California and underneath the paving stones. Veruschka again, elided in truth's wall, her sadness is a quick and aesthetic disappearing thing, mine goes in the place of public space.

The Picture of Sasha Gray

Meaning is sex.
There is no other.

I was born in Sacramento, California.
I never allowed myself to become a product of that environment.

I began college in 2005
balancing school and work seven days a week.

That is when I began thinking about pornography
as a career opportunity.

I was not sexually abused.
I am not on drugs.

The acts I perform are always consensual.
I am a woman who believes in what she does.

I hope to inspire people from all walks of life,
to collaborate with innovative individuals, bohemians welcome.

I grew up in a disenfranchised,
lower-to-middle class neighborhood.

This is not what I preach or believe.

Dan Graham:

The windows projected the outdoor scene onto indoor mirrors, thus multiplying both settings. The mirrors were decorated with silver embossed leaves. When the king arrived, the windows were opened and the sun tinted them into a golden glitter, boasting the king's alchemical ability to turn silver to gold.

The eye must be sun

Ice caked, falling water, compression, clarity, if colors are the deeds and sins of light, this is light caught sleeping. Green abases to gold, red deepens to rouge, a hillside becomes painterly, its grass turns ochre then expires into solidity. A postcard series: the sky painted blue, the grass green, this work is a machinery of distance and contact. Conceptually based sequences, shot North, West, Northwest, Southeast. The mirror is the brightest color; the mirror strikes light.

What proliferates in absence, distance

and is behind every word,

what sounded like lions

but were rips, splices,

the invisible straining toward convexity,

how heaven and death are concurrent

and beauty is a way to appear.

Down under the throne of language

between spectacle and rupture
a ruby spat upon space
a serpentine girl with the head of a bull
who dwells in the plasticity of power unspent
before time is baked into the wall
she organizes radiance,
gesture is a gender
a shining bracelet
which amplifies a slim wrist
super numerary and post sovereign
against all forms of expansion
for all forms of explosion—
superfund solar resonance
makes color, burns color out
makes sense common,
honey in the goldvein of empire
which flows upward from the middle centuries—
reverses direction now
in the basement of her body.

Treatise on Form

Everything within the formal field becomes form. Form feels tactile to the formless, which is unseen, without name, unaccounted for numerically. This is what is meant by economy, the market is in everything. Time is the main concern of form, next, formalizing communication.

When I seek communication, I often find form until I begin speaking in form, and all there is is form, and I seek form when I want exchange. Until there is no inside, until there is only inside, until what's inside is spilling out.

Form is always waiting, intensely feminine, beginning lalations conjoined with emergent textures on screen. Form is slower than growing. Form confronts time. At form's most intense edge, formlessness. At that most intense edge, form.

The question is not which is more powerful, but which is more reproductive. Then, since the terms threaten to flip or reverse, form asks, "is it possible for the formless to reproduce or just spread?" Thus form encodes the definition of reproduction.

Form and light, form and the sun. Communication between objects and light, communication between objects themselves. Perspectival picture space was presaged by boundary lines of cypress trees. This suggests representation is a form of property.

Robert Morris studied engineering at the University of Kansas City and the California School of Fine Arts and earned a master's degree in art history from Hunter College in New York in 1963.

Eva Hesse was a graduate of Yale University School of Fine Arts in 1959.

Nancy Graves received her Master of Fine Arts degree from the Yale School of Art and Architecture in 1964. She traveled in Italy on a Fulbright-Hayes fellowship.

Richard Serra received his Master of Fine Arts degree from Yale in 1964.

Bruce Nauman studied with William Wiley at the University of California at Davis, where he received a Master of Fine Arts degree in 1966.

Robert Ryman received no formal art training. He studied works of art in the collection of the Museum of Modern Art, where he was employed as a guard.

Mierle Laderman Ukeles studied history and international relations before earning her master's degree in creative arts from New York University.

Ann Hamilton graduated from the University of Kansas with a degree in textile design and earned a Master of Fine Arts degree from Yale University School of Fine Arts in 1985.

Martin Puryear studied painting at the Catholic University of America in Washington, DC. He received his Master of Fine Arts degree from Yale in 1971.

Mark Thompson received his Master of Arts degree in sculpture from the University of California at Berkeley in 1973.

During his student years at the Dusseldorf Art Academy, Franz Erhard Walther began to theorize that art is a formless phenomenon solely activated by viewer participation.

Rebecca Horn studied art at the Hochschule Kunste in Hamburg between 1964 and 1970.

The formal age, with its quickness and constant production, demands more and more forms.

Ronaldo Wilson is wearing a mask. Joan Jonas is wearing a mask. Sophia Wang is wearing a mask.

The socius curves around me, glaring. Everything I had spent my life fighting became its sole point: to enter the socius as a form of money.

Representation arises in an ecology of totality.

"Time is elsewhere. Only space exists, infinite and full like a dead stone."

A man gets out of a truck at Fukushima and walks back and forth across a bridge.

This is the form of the formless lament. This mourning does not redirect the dead back into their realm but holds grief inside mercantile walls become an architecture of all systems that killed the sun.

Without name, qualities, masterpiece or practice, fountaining femininity, the formless builds basements of power. Order does not hide disorder, order hides the social.

In reverse of appearance

The plaza is filled with screens, the plaza is filled with pictures. What goes in the absence of a plaza. Sunshine then shadows.

Then ten people, a hundred people, a thousand people, a hundred thousand people fill the plaza. Then ten people, a hundred people, a thousand people, a hundred thousand people hold up a representation. Then ten people, a hundred people, a thousand people, a hundred thousand people stream from the plaza, an agora emptying toward the sun.

In the city in which each communication is already artifact / in the city in which each house is luckier / breathing numbers / in the city in which the city does not exist.

Now the plaza is empty, mute with sun. Then instead of a crowd of 100,000 people, there are 100 crowds of 1,000 people. Then instead of 100 crowds of 1,000 people, there are 10,000 crowds of 10 people.

Here, ten people, a hundred people, a thousand people, a hundred thousand people on screen, become window, renamed for absence. Here, a mother holds up a child turned placard, turned window, turned screen, become sign: a renamed plaza.

At the plaza, a line of police advances. At the plaza, an elder sells cooking oil, boxes of cereal. At the plaza, an agora rendered visible in the Northern California Regional Intelligence Center sensors. Sensing reversed, sense redacted, the redacted rhythm of a plaza.

In which / the plaza was always a representation / turned to look / in the city in which / each house is luckier, breathing numbers / in the city in which / a hundred thousand messages amass and riot / in the city in which / a shadow recomposes identically over every redistribution of forms / in the city in which / the city does not exist / turned to look and my city was gone / at the plaza / the noise of its absence.

A short essay on form

A form amassing. A signal sent and received. An object for use. Form is force. Form behind. Form in a world of radical positivity. Form is leaking. Form learned from limits. Force is form. In this way, form is passive. Form is seen. Light reflects from the surface of form. Form which reforms then dissipates. Form which strikes then flees. Form which curls into being, then uncurls. Now that form is money and language is untied. Signals sounded. Signals rhyme, chime, echo. Form is limit. Form's memory is linguistic. Then written, form conflates with truth. Each law contains elided labor. Which is the bright light of shipwreck signaling other lights. Which is why it is OK to say, "I don't hate form but form's marketplace." Which is why it is OK to say, "I hate form," but not be interested in Organic Form.

I approach the untrained sun and ask,
"how is a field of value different from a factory?"

Common Cinema

Riddem

All the beautiful boys
Have secrets that tie their mouths,
Educations that wind like staircases,
Dressed in pinions, bright as children
In the prison of the collapsed present.

Their speech goes from the mouth as a ribbon,
Stretches out like poverty stretches out in languor,
Records and retells sensory fact that models untellingness,
In collaged rhythmic sequences that
Unfold like the poem but effect change.

In the glittering building, in the self's apartment,
Blossoming in the bright actual library of tears,
They chant, "In the place of absence,
Multiplicity, in the place of givenness,
Repleteness, in the place of languor, rising,
In the place of rhythm, ribbon."

They laugh outside the library,
Read aloud to one another on the pavement.
Actual tears drench the ground. Vast lucid texts
Are unclenched, "It is morning, speech has blossomed,
You are awakening. A lovely light is singing out loud.
In the movement, in my eyes, in the line, Silvia
Federici is alive."

Thatched

shingled, sloped, fixed, patched.
Dirt, concrete, hardwood, lino, washed, scrubbed.
North, South, East, West, cluttered, bare, papered, painted, knocked out, put up.
A-frame, flat. Moss-covered, bricked, tiled, painted, creaking, buckled, floating or
    suspended.
Skeined, silk, paper, disappearing.
Skylights, parties, gardens, landing strips.
Someone else's ceiling, false foundation.
I cannot believe you lied.

Creped skin, pipe smoke, citadel.
Trampled leaves, black dirt, winding path.
I dress this way because I want to.

Sloped, snowcapped.
When it comes down to it, we're talking about money.
Culture is my skin.
At one time I loved him but I believe in him no more.
Checkerboard, parquet, laminate.
Changeable, of questionable consequence.
Philosophy is paramount.
You've taken so much shit.

Insulated, riddled with holes, temporary.

When I was a girl the fireflies signified

I sat on the curb with kids.
In rips and scuffs, eye shining.

I was trapped in amber.
In a sudden Midwest rain.

I laid out flat
in a box of dead differences.

Stunned still
a moth caught in a glass jar.

When I was a beautiful girl,
in a system of ons and offs,

in the silent language of lighthouses,
in an inconsequential, feminine swarm,
the fireflies signified:

One unrolling bolt of ice cream silk, grape sized globes of lapis lazuli and goldvein grouped and reposing in the corners, a fountain or a chandelier, a set of gold combs scalloped in black pearl, a stretched suede book that knocks as soft as a little girl, hautly arched whalebone stilettos, fat, well-behaved chairs, paintings on every inch of ceiling, tiny crystal pots containing notions of mashed lime, birdbath water, temporin and pearl, a leather cup of heron quills, two rocaille tiaras, a Zouave jacket woven from crushed leaves and gold, the extended family of an orchid, a bracelet made of tombstone, a wig culled from Reykvíkingur towheads, a lunar astrolabe, a millefiori flower bed, a set of handwritten encyclopedias, a comprehensive cloud typology, a slice of wedding cake crystallized into chalcedony, a Cherry Plum, Clematis and Honeysuckle cure, a fine and tiny typewriter, porcelain nails in a bell china box, flowers floating in a cabinet vivarium, a perfume of Fiji nectars, a box of San Franciscos.

Cutouts, opulence, piling, pooling at the bottom

heaven is a negative place

a holographic poem, a list

strung on fishing line, of irregularly cut shapes

when you say pleasure, it refers back to the subject

beauty is private, the origin of beauty is private

an open umbrella rising up through sound

when you say sensation, it refers back to the object

a picture has no skin

Dialogue on media and money

for Immanuel Kant

Me and the landlord across the table in the toxic kitchen
when I thought I would be out on the street with my daughter,

him laughing, we are here now, not alone,
this is how you are not alone.

Finally, this sense between us,
perfectly communicable, entirely illuminated.

This house prevents singularity, he said.
Once you become media, you are never alone.

Me and him across the table
when I thought I would be out on the street,

him laughing at me, here we are together,
this is how you get to be not alone.

A structure for the singular body, I thought,
a crib, a coffin, a visible interval in appearances.

Here on the table: a sense between us
and no way out of making it.

There was a fight scene

The father was shirtless and so was the son.
They were outdoors in the sun of a dying day.
It was green and late summer.
His jaw is opened.
"There is blood on your hands."
The father stops to slick a strand of hair
from the son's eyes.
Garlic, onion, a big boat of human smells,
a deed, a property,
a beautiful girl,
a city, a governor, a business booming.
The son could win
by ducking and dancing
were not the father the mother's lover.

They fight your snake with a long stick

while you stand at a cocktail party and watch.
The snake makes image upon image
and you call out an interpretation.
The walls are painted white.
Interpretation converts the whiteness into value,
now it is a screen.
Property is not about possession as much as value,
you stir your drink and think,
the language which organizes sensation—

Common Cinema

It was in picturesque Cherbourg
that the sickness of the singular found me again

in that communicative picture
of a thing made not to communicate its labor,

a thing lost to the assembly line
which now pervades the office and the emotional streets.

In the cinema you're low voicing utopia
to the young woman sitting next to you

you hum to her
everything blue and not yet written upon,

communication is the girlish labor
that turns this factory on.

Eleanor Antin

An airhorn recomposes light—

a sense is thrown—

dawn breaks amidst a phone call—

a big copper sound—

and each leaf turns

toward the screen's greedy light

a field of free speech

disappearing to thumbtacks—

I write from this poem

which is a camera

in which I compose myself.

Fe-

She takes a series of full body percepts, she files them in a shoebox, she gets them made into slides and projects them onto city surfaces. They are accosting and replacing normal flow, creating an inward space externally and thus reproducing thousands of like inward spaces aligned conceptually with femininity, and thus fecundity.

The moon is the first cinema (Forever 21)

In a clasped box made of mother-of-pearl
containing all my baby's teeth
the moon witnessed what I went through last week.
I could not forget, Moon,
the way you nonconsensually took my body
then released it to the night.
My baby slept across the bridge
clasped inside our gender
while you, Moon,
with only a face that hides, then comes out,
with pearlescent purple lipstick,
Moon, babe, I don't accept your wordless apology,
you bright bitch of luck,
you hockey puck,
you dear and pockmarked star.

"I cannot cry,"

said the Sun
with a violucent
looked-at-ness,
"femininity is a messy jungle of light,"
throwing sense around like
a shawl or cape,
"art's a heap
let's sleep."

Sun Cycle

I.

One city constructs another city in reverse,
a thousand windows open, an immediate and disappearing library.
The sun's a creep this week.
Force transforms form at exceptional velocity;
I will arise from this accelerated archeology to spit in knowing's eye.

II.

I wanted to throw the sun in the trash can,
I wanted its second nature.
I wanted to understand form's mimicry,
I dreamed of sexual violence too,
walking from gallery to junk store;
on everyone's computer screen that week
everything everywhere walking right through.

III.

The sun smashes me.
It unpetals me.
The sun slides its eyes all around me.
The sun reveals me, unearned.
The sun sorts me, battles me, surrounds
and impregnates me.
The sun is my main respondent.

IV. Nouns by Bataille, compiled for Elliot Rodger

thing is
parody is
thing is
form

body is
sun is
vehicle is
frenzy

lead is
parody is
gold is
parody is
coitus is
parody is
crime

origin is
ground is
base is
center

car is
clock is
machine is
image

sentence is
tracings is

system is
centers is
circles is
totality is
labyrinth

shoe is
tooth is
nose is
love

smell is
eggs is
eyes is
root is
love

dog is
stomach is
goose is
woman is
jar is
confusion is
vehicle is
love

earth is
animal is
man is
result is
cause is
animal is

man is
earth is
coitus

man is
others is
one is
others

girl is
presence is
it is
darkness

love is
vanity is
diamond is
rage is
image is
mirror

I is
indifference is
her is
me is
I is
love is
her is
she is
I is
her is
she is
forgetting

forgetting is
subterfuge

man is
specter is
coffin

direction is
sun is
ground

tree is
ground is
shaft is
sun

tree is
lightning is
ground is
love

love is
cloud is
cloud is
earth is
storm is

the only rain was falling stones

sun is
hand is
tree is
eye

erection is
sun is
cellar

eye is
sun is
cadavers is
reaction

face is
passion is
debauchery is
indecency

nothing is
entrails

ground is
water

idea is
force is
eruption

organ is
parts is
eruption

deflagrations is
heavens

fertility is
disaster

love is
throat

parody is
blinding sun

I am the filthy parody
of the torrid and blinding sun

I is
throat is
girl is
I

you is
night

I is
throat is
girl
you are the night

you are
throat is
girl is
the night

blinding is
violating is

night is
sun

blinding is
sun is
you are
night

sun is
empire is
no sun
sets ever

A slow motion running slide into a slick of yellow acrylic, then two bare feet are received into mouths of sun.

Soliloquy

Go on

This story starts with a stripper
or some kind of exhibitionist
bending over in a gold body suit;
a big heart covers most of the screen
and Hole's song "Violet" plays softly.

The day was aflame like the seal got ripped off the top of a Pringles can,
I emerged from your room,
around my head an invisible plume.

The kind of oneness they share
describes the overall existence of life on earth
with the elements water and fire
giving them a fulfilling experience that lasts
till the time they can walk in the eternity of their love.

I awoke from a dream. I was about to give you head.
Your bedroom was in the back of the house,
beyond the window was an ocean.
The city moved through us in canals of separation.
Everywhere hovered like pollen,
permanent dereliction.

I felt a sense of desperation until I found a weapon.
I had gone back into the wood, over the plants,
leaping from big stone to big stone then up a mountain
made of stones till I got a flat gray shale shiv,
sharp at both ends, perfect for my hand.

It did not attempt to conquer me,
but I would never match its size.
I couched, I bowed, I stretched out my paws,
laid them flat, named it an object of the sublime.

I cycle around the internet looking for you all night,
and the sky was made of amethyst,
and all the stars look just like little fish,
I find you looking at Tumblr porn
I still have a link to your likes.

The morning is bathed in digital radiance,
I yawn insensate into ornate violence.
almost-too-pretty slutty-and-cute 2-or-more-girls-is-a-party
master-of-o watching-my-husband tit-fux-and-cumshots just-young-feet hells-cuties
clueless-boyfriend stepmothers milf-bondage.

I dreamed there was shortage.
Each family had to pick one.
My father killed me by saying *you're dead*
I was horizontal and floating through my house
I could see and hear everyone
but no one could see or hear me.

Now pink sparkles stream from her throat
and the stripper paints back on her clothes—
she squirts two dropperfuls of blue nail polish
from the tincture bottle into her mouth.

"I never said Courtney killed him
I don't know if that's the case or not
don't don't know if that's the case or not"

"she is younger than you
and doesn't have a child
young younger than you
and doesn't have a child
she is younger than you and doesn't have a child"
"your big brother was just such a beautiful boy
I always wondered why no one fussed over the baby—"

La Brea, almost too pretty, stretches out in unfathomable infinity,
an airplane overhead trails a banner,
"who can alchemize empire inside their own body?"

I walk to the river.
I'm going to live forever.
I gather dead flowers and rotted mice,
my hair down around my waist.
I want to be encased.
Diamonds and rubies fall from my mouth,
noir nets of shadow cast over me.
The succulent visual object
encrusted in smashed address
renders the self an evanescent reference point;
the eye is gaped by the screen,
go on take everything—

Sun to moon

In the middle of the story is a black cobra,
a barbed hula hoop,
an angel in her mouth,
two hands in her mouth,
desire is a piston in her mouth;
this full, this is fertile
is precious and minor,
display an angel in her mouth
climb into hands in her mouth
choke it in your hands
close its eyes toward the light
fold it into a conquered city
expectorate desire is a piston in her mouth.

Leave a shell like a wrapping
which is the imprint of force, abandoned

I had risen bigger than my body
in perpetual reproduction

address my body
all address, turn to poison

three pale flowers on the ground
within the administration of fire

within silver
within the administration of soft medicine

within soft rope
within windows

I will awake every one of my fifteen powers
where they cry from the ground to be found

now I feel my gravity, but I have no money

I could not appropriate my own gold snake
I went South but I could not maintain

all shadow's up for debate inside this box of ghosts

soft black rope, underbraid, water, fire, little rope,
dead leaf curled 'round a flower

the dream was an aviary of color

I will renounce my love
I will put it in the bottom drawer

I put my beauty in the bottom drawer.

I always keep my head above my body. That rapist of mine was on the wrong side of history. Slow trap, dirt garage, surfeit giving birth to new industry, a notebook of noise, a misprision of interiority. Soft clanking medicines: oh slow cobweb, the city today is hysterical with masculinity, the city is a brave green canyon within an administration of fire. Mirrors upon mirrors, mirrors heaped upon mirrors. Mirrors upon mirrors, mirrors upon mirrors, mirrors upon mirrors, mirrors heaped upon mirrors. Mirrors upon mirrors upon mirrors upon mirrors, mirrors heaped upon mirrors, mirrors upon mirrors. I am taken by black birds, the sky is missing where they fly. A deep dark blue whip, an imperial country, the sun all diffuse, wail me down, mirrors heaped upon mirrors, wail me down, my thick riches, wail me down, a black balloon flames out, abolishment: one note flies like a long, vulnerable flag. I reach for my flag, I reach for my fetish.

What if I come to you with a mouth full of black stones?
What if there is a snake in the back of my throat?
What if I fill up my cheeks with sun and blow sun into your eyes?
What if I spit out each syllable of your body one by one
until you appear
and this is my bright new song.

Then a cloud

put their hand over my mouth, then a butterfly wing struck my cheek, then the excess gathered into a photograph and that was love, a silver volcano turning red. Then they put their arms above their head to protect it like a baby's head, I put their excess to use, checked their gender, then they crawled to my breast, put my excess to use, a silver volcano, a silver volcano.

Then they pulled my arms and legs in four directions and I came apart like bread or butter, then I was a thing like a southern ocean, a thing like a field of ragweed, like a pincushion of satin, a strand of Aryan hair, and then a thing outside these things, a thing in darkness which is also coldness, a thing unreadable or impossible to sort through, a thing suspended in pure potentiality, an imprint of disorganization, everything counter to social life, everything too soft to have appeared.

When they looked at me with masculine eyes, gardens sprung forth from my belly. Then they looked at me with dead eyes, and genders sprung forth from my body. Then time shot up from a fountain in the middle of their town and became cumulus in the sky. The little town passing its clouds and festivals, a steady stream of books passing under the library sensor down the street. Then light gathered and then dissolved. I thought we might detach a silver social life from its territory of gold. Then they opened their eyes like a butterfly's wet wings. Then the foliage, perpetually green.

The book of this

The book of this is dark and compact.
It has an ornate cover which is thick, embossed, or encrusted.
The book of this has yellowed pages with writing so small
it is nearly illegible.
The book of this repels its reader.
It is physically hard to open, like a weapon.
The book of this book is so very private.
This book looks like reversal.
This book has a beauty that's ruined when it's read.

To describe ascension through the century

and its ideals, down through the city, into the club on its bedrock of the negative, with its dissonant noise, and comfortably inverted there, shining like a diamond in a blue headscarf, like a terrorist in the permanently inverted feminine, smiling in the teeth, winning in the gaze, a decade turns upon this fulcrum, having careened without regulation and stopped here to preen and have a look around. If its work was aesthetic life, this was its bad perfect moment, then this character bats two pair of eyelashes in slow motion, lets go gestalt, absorbing noise, richened by riches, there was a manifesto for this, oh silent strange crash, oh rained upon street.

The Picture of Dorian Gray (at 16 frames per second)

The sunlight slipped over the polished leaves. In the grass, white daisies were tremulous. The spray of lilac fell from his hand upon the gravel. A furry bee came and buzzed round it for a moment. In the slanting beams that streamed through the open doorway the dust danced and was golden. The heavy scent of roses seemed to brood over everything. Some large blue china jars and parrot-tulips were ranged on the mantelshelf, and through the small leaded panes of the window streamed the apricot-coloured light of a summer day in London. The sunset had smitten into scarlet gold the upper windows of the houses opposite. The panes glowed like plates of heated metal. The sky above was like a faded rose. The tulip beds across the road flamed like throbbing rings of fire. A white dust, tremulous cloud of orris-root it seemed, hung in the panting air. The brightly-colored parasols danced like monstrous butterflies. The darkness lifted, and, flushed with faint fires, the sky hollowed itself into a perfect pearl. Huge carts filled with nodding lilies rumbled slowly down the polished empty street. The sky was pure opal now, and the roofs of the houses glistened like silver against it. From some chimney opposite a thin wreath of smoke was rising. It curled, a violet riband, through the nacre coloured air.

Attributions

All sentences but one in "The Picture of Sasha Gray" are taken from actor and artist Sasha Gray's Myspace page. Gray, who from ages 18–21 performed in and produced pornographic films, took her name from the character in Oscar Wilde's novel *The Picture of Dorian Gray.*

"Dan Graham:" quotes from a 2013 artist lecture by Dan Graham at the San Francisco Art Institute.

The line "Time is elsewhere. Only space exists, infinite and full like a dead stone" is from Leslie Kaplan's *Excess—The Factory,* Commune Editions, 2014. It appears in "Everything within the formal field becomes form."

The litany of artists' educational credentials in "Everything within the formal field becomes form" is taken variously from Kristine Stiles's entry in *Theories and Documents of Contemporary Art: A Sourcebook of Artist Writings,* marked in the index under "anti-form."

The reference to cypress trees, property lines, and the discovery of perspectival space is Henri Lefebvre's theory from his book *The Production of Space.*

The phrase "Common Cinema" is the name for non-institutional film workshops created by critic and professor Louis-Georges Schwartz.

The line "a camera / in which I compose myself" from "Eleanor Antin" describes Antin's 1972 video *Representational Painting,* in which the artist puts on a full face of makeup while staring into the camera lens.

All words in part IV of the section "Sun Cycle," "Nouns by Bataille, complied for Elliot Rodger," are from the essay "L'anus Solaire" by George Bataille. I identified every noun and arranged them in (mostly) consecutive order. One line from Etel

Adnan's *The Arab Apocalypse*, "the only rain was falling stones," is interjected into the list. Elliot Rodger killed six people and injured fourteen others near the campus of the University of California, Santa Barbara, in 2014. A manifesto he left behind described hatred of women and racialized people; he claimed his half-Caucasian British heritage entitled him to attention from women.

The line "go on take everything" is from the 1994 Hole song "Violet."

"*The Picture of Dorian Gray* (at 16 frames per second)" catalogs every line of description in Oscar Wilde's 1890 novel in consecutive order.

Other sources include Elaine Scarry's *On Beauty and Being Just*; Immanuel Kant's *Critique of Judgment* (translated by Werner S. Pluhar); Tiqqun's *Raw Materials for a Theory of the Young-Girl* (2001 edition, translated anonymously) and "Sonogram of a Potential" (translated anonymously); the Bernadette Corporation film *Get Rid of Yourself*; Arthur Schopenhauer's *The World as Will and Representation* (translated by E.F.J. Payne); Jean Baudrillard's *Simulacra and Simulation* (translated by Sheila Faria Glaser); Stephen Shore's 2012 lecture at the San Francisco Museum of Modern Art; Juhani Pallasmaa's *The Eyes of the Skin*; Denise Levertov's *Some Notes on Organic Form*; George Oppen's "Of Being Numerous"; Ted Berrigan's "Sonnet XXXVII"; an interview with the Northern California chief of riot control on NPR, 2013; a Facebook post by Tooth; and a comment poet Zoe Tuck made at a poetics talk Barrett Watten gave at Brian Ang's house, 2011.

The epigraph is from Monique Wittig's experimental novel *The Lesbian Body* (translated by David Le Vay), Beacon Press, 1973.

All other epigraphs are composed by the author.

Acknowledgments

Thank you CA Conrad, Dawn Lundy Martin, Caryl Pagel, and Hilary Plum. Dear thanks to all readers of this book in various forms, Shandy Walton, Ivy Johnson, and Ted Rees. Gratitude to the art spaces and presses who supported its development, Jasmine Moorhead of Krowswork Gallery, Margaret Tedesco of [2nd Floor Projects], and Gazing Grain Press.

Some of these poems appear in the chapbook *from a Book of Poems on Beauty*, which won the 2014 Gazing Grain Award, supported by George Mason University. Some appear in an untitled double chapbook with Lara Durbeck published by Supersuperette.

"You awaken to ornate, administrative violence," "Pollen," "Command poem" and "The soil is" appeared in the *Chicago Review*, Fall 2016, editor Andrew Peart.

"An unaccountable beauty" and "Fronding and intricate" appeared in *Fence*, Winter/Spring 2015, editor Rebecca Wolff.

"Before we were filled with content, we sought to be filled with sensation" appeared in *Try* magazine, 2010, editors David Brazil and Sara Larsen, and in *Action, Yes!*, Winter 2011, as part of an excerpt of *from A Book of Poems on Beauty*, editors Johannes Göransson and Joyelle McSweeney. "When I was a girl the fireflies signified," "There was a beautiful fight scene," and "One unrolling bolt" appeared in *Action, Yes!* as well. The latter was commissioned by artist Sydney Hermant for inclusion in her artist book *Aunt Maude's Scrapbook*, published by JRP Ringier in 2006.

"Pollen" and "Command poem," as well as the full section "Sun Cycle," appeared in *Armed Cell* 8 as part of an excerpt titled "Sun Cycle," editor Brian Ang.

"The natural world frozen" forms the basis of the final artwork made by artist Sonya Rappoport (d. 2015). Her installation *The Transitive Property of Equality* consists of a game based on the lines of this poem as well as collaged works on paper with text, Krowswork Gallery, 2015. It was anthologized in *It's Night in San Francisco But It's Sunny in Oakland*, Timeless Infinite Light, 2014, as was "In reverse of appearance" and "My mother was a secret house."

"My mother was a secret house," "Common Cinema," and "Then a cloud," appeared in *Open House*, volume 2, number 1, editor Ivy Johnson.

"The eye must be sunlight," "Riddem," and "What proliferates in absence, distance" appeared in *Where Eagles Dare*, Summer 2014, editor Steve Orth.

"Down under the throne of language" was exhibited on the wall at Southern Exposure Gallery in San Francisco, California, in August 2016, curators Patricia Maloney and Valerie Imus. The poem was also in *Eleven Eleven*, issue 22, editor Hugh Behm-Steinberg.

"Everything within the formal field becomes form" documents a sound piece created for a residency at Krowswork Gallery in February 2015, curator Jasmine Moorehead. [2nd Floor Projects] Gallery published a different version as a limited edition in October 2015, curator Margaret Tedesco. *Art Practical* reprinted it in March 2016, editors Matt Sussman and Brandon Brown.

"A short essay on form" appeared in the San Francisco Museum of Modern Art's *Open Space*, editor Suzanne Stein. "In reverse of appearance" was originally commissioned by Suzanne as part of an essay to accompany a 2013 SECA Award site-specific artwork. It was recorded for the KQED Litography Project radio show about Occupy Oakland.

"The book of this" appeared in *Dusie* 15, editor Carrie Hunter.

"Go on" appeared in *Elderly* 16, editors Jamie Townsend and Nicholas DeBoer.

"Sun to moon" is a performance text with video, performed so far at the Poetic Research Bureau, Amy's Kitchen Reading Series, and Artist's Access Television.

"I always keep my head above my body" appeared in the *Scribbler's Quarterly*, Fall 2018, editor DeWayne Dickerson.

"Then a cloud" formed the text for a video piece titled *Olympia*, which appeared in *Gauss PDF*, issue 215, editor Gordon Faylor. *Olympia* also screened at Krowswork Gallery in 2016, curator Jasmine Moorhead, and appeared as "Olympia" in *Open House*, volume 2, issue 1.

Other portions of this work appeared in chapbooks for the Dusie Kollektiv (2011) and Supersuperette press (2014).

This book is dedicated to Kathleen Fraser, 1935–2019.

Anne Lesley Selcer is the author of the essay collection *Blank Sign Book* and *from A Book of Poems on Beauty*, winner of the Gazing Grain Press Award. Her writing on art includes *Banlieusard*, a book-length text for Artspeak, as well as essays for museum and gallery catalogs and art magazines. Writing occasionally manifests as moving image or sound. It is included in several anthologies, most recently *New Media Art 2017* from the CICA Museum.